If I Didn't Love the River

PREVIOUS WORKS

Love is Hard (CD Baby, 2022)

BAAM! (CD Baby, 2018)

Missing Piece (Dundurn Press, 2017)

The Wolf Is Back (Wolsak & Wynn, 2017)

Second Kiss (Dundurn Press, 2015)

The Paper Sword (Dundurn Press, 2014)

Previously Feared Darkness (ECW Press, 2014)

Rosa Rose (Wolsak & Wynn, 2013)

Feeling the Pinch (CD Baby, 2012)

Reading the Bible Backwards (ECW Press, 2008)

How to Swallow a Pig (ECW Press, 2004)

Blue Pyramids: Selected Poems (ECW Press, 2002)

The Secret Invasion of Bananas (Cherubim Press, 1999)

Resurrection in the Cartoon (ECW Press, 1997)

Tongue 'n' Groove (Artisan Music, 1997)

The Time Release Poems (Ekstasis, 1997)

If I Didn't Love the River

POEMS

Robert Priest

Published by ECW Press
665 Gerrard Street East
Toronto, Ontario, Canada M4M 1Y2
416-694-3348 / info@ecwpress.com

Editor for the Press: Michael Holmes / a misFit book
Copy editor: Emily Schultz
Cover design: Jessica Albert
Author photo: Allen Booth

MISFIT

LIBRARY AND ARCHIVES CANADA CATALOGUING IN PUBLICATION

Title: If I didn't love the river : poems / Robert Priest.

Other titles: If I did not love the river

Names: Priest, Robert, 1951- author.

Identifiers: Canadiana (print) 20220226334 | Canadiana (ebook) 20220226369

ISBN 978-1-77041-694-9 (softcover)
ISBN 978-1-77852-050-1 (ePub)
ISBN 978-1-77852-051-8 (PDF)
ISBN 978-1-77852-052-5 (Kindle)

Classification: LCC PS8581.R47 I4 2022 | DDC C811/.54—dc23

The publication of *If I Didn't Love the River* has been generously supported by the Canada Council for the Arts and is funded in part by the Government of Canada. *Nous remercions le Conseil des arts du Canada de son soutien. Ce livre est financé en partie par le gouvernement du Canada.* We acknowledge the support of the Ontario Arts Council (OAC), an agency of the Government of Ontario, which last year funded 1,965 individual artists and 1,152 organizations in 197 communities across Ontario for a total of $51.9 million. We also acknowledge the contribution of the Government of Ontario through the Ontario Book Publishing Tax Credit, and through Ontario Creates for the marketing of this book.

This book is dedicated to my beloved,
Marsha Kirzner,
and to the memory of my father,
Edward Priest
(December 15, 1928 to June 25, 2022).

This book remembers my brothers in song,
Graeme Williamson and Peter Lafferty;
my brother in poetry, Robert Sward;
and the very generous Sherrie Gatenby.

Contents

Love Has Nothing to Do

Love has nothing to do with the stars
except that I see them as symbols of distance
and love can be distant

It has nothing to do with rivers
but I see the river staying and going
and I remember that love leaves and remains

Love is not much swayed by the moon
but who can view the moon
and not think of love's satellite tendencies
its shadowy diminishments

True fire — the flame is not love
but in its dance, in the light it sheds
we see what we become
when love is in us

If I Didn't Love the River

If I didn't love the river
how could I say I love you
If I didn't wish for the world to thrive
If I didn't work to change minds
that wouldn't be love
I love you because I love tomorrow
and I want to keep it just a day away forever
If I saw hunger and didn't dream of a feast
If I didn't dream of children well-nourished
what would nourish my love
What would my longing for peace grow fat on
My love of justice is all wound up in my love for you
It wouldn't be love if I didn't love creatures running free
if I didn't support the right of others to love
It wouldn't be love if I gave away my voice
so others could add it to the mob
There has to be work to it, there has to be vision
If I didn't love the scorned, the othered
If I didn't love the children of war
how could I truly say I love anyone

Confession

I love you
weakly sickly
with hands that will be dust
A ghost
with songs
that are not hits
My love so weak
it cannot make you last
beyond your time
more than a thousand years

I love you
temporarily
for only so long
as I live
Only so long
as I have breath
Only to
the very door of death
And only since I first saw you
not before

My love so limited
I freely give
ephemeral
a mist
of countable kisses
A stretch of vibes
no more

Between a Tender and a Tender Place

Between a tender and a tender place
I wait for you, sensing your moment's near.
With abandon rising in your voice
you groan out loud. You're free — no one can hear.
We slide in and out of being. We strobe
to our extremes and back in luscious arcs
till stardust starts to tingle in our toes.
Redoubled rhythms triple in the dark
as though our thudding pelvises were flint
whose soft impacts could only strike a spark
colliding at a superhuman rate.
At last a flash ignites the lamps beneath our skins
and I collapse on you. We pant and grin.
"Don't come out yet," you whisper, "please stay in."

On Star Divination

We are devices thrown down by the stars
divining sticks with no will of our own
Our bodies where they land leave marks
which can, they say, prefigure the unknown
The shapes we make, the forms we take at birth
how wide at times ecstatic limbs are spread —
all such random prints in water and in earth
are auguries if they can just be read
Some stars disdain all such beliefs and yet
they roll the dice — ironically — again . . . again
We are their guilty pleasure alphabet
We're lots cast down relentlessly like rain
We guide them home when they are lost, our love so luminous
they can't avert their eyes. And yes, oh yes — stars wish on us

I Want to Go Back

I want to go back
and love her from afar as a child

I want to love her as a teenager
all those years before I knew her

when she was too tall
and I was too small

I want to return to the chance I had
when I was twenty-two and walked away

not knowing
I had a chance

I want to re-taste
our first kiss

relive
my first afternoon with her

reride that bed that field
up against that tree

If I could get back to that night
When I wrote "Poem for a Tall Woman"

I would and we would make love exactly as we did
and I would write the poem again just as it is

So Close

Here is where the heart is
where the hand is
here is where the vow is

depending on what
"here" we mean

Here in this home
Here on the street
in this country
Here in the world
in the universe

We are certainly somewhere

You are there
and I am also there
depending on who's speaking
and what time it is
Depending on how we identify
the limits of moment

All I know is
there is some reaching
required
some receiving
called for
some distance
to be overcome
before we can be
close

How close?
So close
we intersect
So close
the light has hardly left one of us
before the other
is illuminated

Love Lets Love Shout

Love lets love shout
Love allows love to gripe and whine

When love lives with love
expect the squeal of friction

smooth and rough
somehow combined

To mix it up requires
mutually sensitized action

Love is both the stick
and the word stirred by the stick

It is the spin
and the yang and the yin

hurled to the rim
of love's double orbit

"Yes to little collisions," yells love
"Yes to incandescence"

Love allows love up from its place
beneath the feet

What was not, now becomes
fountain, foam, a thrill that flickers

in two bodies with one
snake tongue

Yes love allows the stereo
probe of the forked universe

to be undone in the twin
nodes of we two

clinging to twigs
of each other in the tide

amazed our identities
survive

Misunderstanding

We've dropped the language
repeatedly
It's all been shattered and put back together
so many times
by complete amateurs it's just a mishmash
the syllables jammed, jarred
crammed together, bits stuck on other bits
all wrong, a Frankenstein smorgasbord
a crockery convention in earthquake season

Some bull keeps romping through the china shop
and language, pretty language, topples
Gravity has pulled down words and they
all lie agglomerated in maniacal mosaics
bleeding an unspeakable melange
of meaningless connection
as though all puzzles and glues
had been dumped here
in one lexicon
and a fan turned on
Every vocable a quilt
a polyglot flag
unravelled by speaking

Somebody has fucked up the words
and they all have meaningless bits
The rain has worn them down
Love has hurt them
They have cracked open
and been bled dry

It would be better to just make faces
or shrug and walk away
It would be better if we did not speak
for a while

Seeking Itself

Seeking itself
magnetic north repels
magnetic north

Jason drives the golden fleece
further away with each thrust of the oars

This great mission to put a man on the horizon

The magnifier burning the map
the map igniting the territory
the ship poisoning the sea

The bullseye shifty
you can't know where it is

Only by not looking
only by closing the eyes
only by shutting down the investigation

If there is a search
the police will wind up in each other's arms
the disappeared more and more disappeared

Truth slips away
before the finger

In search of our humanity
we commit the atrocity of step after step

They Won't Stay In

They won't stay in, the things I must not say.
I stuff them in a box. I lock the vault
but my skin splits — tries to scream anyway.
I beg for medicine, they rub in salt
And seal it over locking in the lie.
I've been shamed silent by a cruel command.
But not this time. I reach out my red hand
and lifting up the lid let slip just one thin cry —
one cry of agony so long denied
but in that cry are ten more stifled cries
each one with ten more stifled cries inside.
In exponential waves they multiply.
The truth explodes whoever's world it rocks.
No one resists for long Pandora's box.

Egalitarian

I hardly dare to wish for freedom from
my troubles before fear of irony
stops me cold. Yes you'll be free old chum —
and then the nasty ending comes.

You know — as in Oedipus plucks his eyes.
Shouldn't I rather wish for my fair share
of troubles? That's the egalitarian way.
But then I stop to do the math — take care

Add up the pain of modern slavery —
of child mortality, of those in jails
and old age homes, of refugees and all the agony
of poverty — then put my own upon the scale.

A staggering sum — which I divide by . . . what?
A mere eight billion? Think I'll stick with what I've got.

Depression

Like wave and water I'd move on and stay —
while sun reflections warp, distort, and clash
But in a maelstrom waves by waves are dashed away
and scattered in the wind's deranging wrath

Just so my thoughts are shattered by each thought
They burst and break, they flood and then recede
In panic they go off all scattershot
That's where I live, that's where my senses feed —

The fury on the fury, fear on fear
in havoc that descends to every shore
My currents cross, collide, and disappear
and I am sucked down to the ocean floor

A pressure creature crushed by gravity
No will, no way, no hope, no agency

Why I See a Therapist

Everything reminds me
of the Third Reich

When I see an image of Hitler
I think I'm looking in a mirror

My neighbour puts up a little fence
and all I see is barbed wire

Behind the most precision elocutions
I detect a slight German accent

When trains moan at night
I turn away and shudder

Any little corporal with a head injury
Anyone interested in twins

All modern media —
Goebbels Goebbels Goebbels

All your high art
Nazi art

Jets overhead
V2s Luftwaffe

When silence persists
it is always that silence

Even when the priest says mass
my brain adds "murder"

The word concentration
makes me think of camps

I see libraries
as bonfires to be

Corporations expand and I have to
plug my ears Lebensraum Lebensraum

Every cross, every logo
hides a swastika

My name in nightmares
is Quisling

All democracies
Weimar Republics

Native reservations
a slower holocaust

When terrible things are not said outright
I understand exactly what we all agree to do

Boots tramp up the street at night and
I think haystack, I think pogrom

I think will I say
"But I'm not a Jew"

I fear the gold in my own teeth
My wife's long hair a death warrant

Would I be the one
who collects spectacles

Will I be one of those
who says we didn't know, none of us knew

Every time we rewrite history
I splinter off with it

Into that alt world
where Hitler triumphed

I'm either ashes
or torchbearer

My poems propaganda
My songs new servile anthems

If they play "O Canada" and I stand
the lyrics are always "Sieg Heil Sieg Heil"

My upright stance as I sing along
a straight-armed salute

Amnesia

I forgot
how memory gapes
at the wrists
how memory
twists the rag
of the throat
I forgot how much
a kick
a foot could be
how much a fist
a stomach is

I forgot
the broken-nosed blood-breath
the crooked finger
ringing
when the blade bit

I forget
that I am a man
that I am a woman
a child born
of rage
a fetus expanding into
lost shape

I do not remember
the clang
of a stone palm
smash to the face

I have no recollection
of impact again and again

Something spilled the puzzle
of memory
the pieces sucked back
into the embodied black
abyss

Lightning took my amygdala
my frontal lobe

I used to know all about forgetting
but now I only remember
the angel voltage
of instantaneity

No more flashbacks

Even impermanence
eludes me
I grab at it
like flame
at a moth
my childhood goes down
a kamikaze butterfly
flapping to ignition

But how long can I remain an axletree
cut loose
from the burning spokes
of attachment

The past starts
developing
slowly at first
like a photograph
but then it rushes in

The flies come back
The fridge hums
My father swivels around angry
My mother leers back
over her shoulder
The ancestors
with knowing eyes
grinning from
long black rooms

Name It Ghazal

This darkness in a pain-free zone. Name it.
It haunts my throat, its cause unknown. Name it.

Cadaver-cold, it crooks my fingers round
another's blood dark in my own. Name it.

A dog electro-shocked from years of sleep
is shrieking through my hollow bones. Name it.

An inverse sun that tugs horizons down
to read the grave's unwritten stone. Name it.

The rotting meat of angel suicide,
The straw-thick wrist its wound unsewn. Name it.

The gaslit seer, the murdered god.
The staked moth shuddering alone. Name it.

The unborn twin still stunted in my chest
screams to me its soul ingrown. Name it.

A faceless priest in dry baptism chants
but can't, in his unholy tone, name it.

I rob this ritual. I derail it.
I know fear. I've always known. I name it.

Another Victim of Grammar

Another victim of grammar
the word writhes in its wrack

It would tell you anything
It would swear that things aren't separate

Every word betrays its language
eventually

When they are tortured
words scream like birds

They shriek like women
They snap like men

Only when they finally signify nothing
are they thrown back to the mouths of the mob

Whose joyous shouts
give them terrible new meaning

Device

You read me to sleep at night
and in the morning wake me up
First thing in my pocket when I dress
you tell me the time
the weather
You're my guitar tuner
my recorder when I sing
If I want to know anything it's you I ask
You recognize my voice my face
intimate whorls of fingerprints, thumbprints
If I fibrillate you warn me
connect me to my father my mother my friends
my corporations
I hardly need a memory, you store
the essentials
clock calendar magnifier
all my favourites at my fingertips
You count each step each breath when I walk
and when I dance
you show me the moves
speak my language in any voice I choose
always listening noting my likes and dislikes
my hits and misses
leaving my pen to lie fallow
you turn my voice to text
and then autocorrect

You're my compass sermon
church and brothel
broadcasting my virtues
filtering my inadequacies
All that's fed to you is fed to me and I select

film poetry gossip science
I catch the world, the sky, and freeze-frame it
visit far-off catastrophes
radiate empathy through you
A portal to purchase
all the goods of the earth
and you draw them to me
make a magnet of my home

Before they are gone forever I can identify
the flora, the fauna
face-to-face with distant friends
you shrink distances
adjust the heat, prompt the oven
guard the door, light the way
My guru when I meditate
fact checker jukebox peephole spirit level omniscient window
You lead me to the roads less travelled
and pay my bills
tracking my screen time calibrating stop lights, street lights
gauging gas pumps, adjusting speeds
Polyglot Babel box memory wafer
the weapons await your discretion
where free speech runs wild
refaithing the faithless linking like to like
domino to domino
info to input, lie to sucker, mark to grifter
A centrifuge to separate light from heavy
right from left
vaxxed from un
A world for the worldless

You make the micro macro
suck us in and beam us out

Hypnotist's medallion
slippery fish bank note
needle eye
soul scan
rabbit hole
passport
data fix
opiate eye

We charge you
and you charge us
fix us to the grid
nail us up to interstices
rivet us in bits
drone bait
glitter box
pocket cuff
mallard tag

You are the finger for all pies
And we can't quit you

You fasten
flies to the web
and make them pay

The Like Process

I just stand back here and reel in the likes
I pull in my nets wriggling with likes
The likes come at me like geese from all countries
Fluttering likes, roosting butterfly-like likes
They come at me quickly like iron filings
to the magnet
Branches full of black crows
sitting darkly

I like these likes
These likes that fall from afar
like toppled obelisks
like overturned statues
plummeting down
all to one point

My ribs are twigs where likes perch each by each
Likes in long long rows
Likes land like flying ants
on long black bones
one like dragging in two more
and two more and two more

There are likes that like other likes now
And other likes that like the likes that like likes

The likes come at me
like shuttles
to a mothership
The way flies
flock to a corpse
and I am a like hive

I am a like machine
They zero in out of corners
They sponge up out of cracks
Octopus-like likes insincere likes
seeking favour
Like-drones swarming the bullseye
stretching the new like metric
to reach peak like

Like reduction
Less and less likes
A minimum number of likes please
Empty likes
Likes you don't like
that mean nothing to you
Not one like
Likeless
The end of like

Big Money

Big money is a money magnet
it draws itself
to itself
so fast it rips holes in the chest, in families

A syringe sucking
at the flesh of the hungry
it drains blood from veins
The needle sinking deeper
right through the bottom
into the next child and the next
drawing youth from youth
sucking truth dry
leaving only the lie the big lie

No one vault can contain it
Big money grows bigger and bigger
spending itself on itself
hiding itself in itself
Big money fraks people
drains the human aquifer
extracting brain and spittle
spinal fluid
sucking will from will

Money gravity
tugs the clouds down
drags the rain into the needle eye
stripping fur off animals
leaching the ovum from the egg

And those who have not been eviscerated
keep waiting for the draw to end
for wealth to be big enough for any one man
for the gout of blood to stop snowballing

But money keeps flying to money
knocking down its own walls
accreting offshore
bursting up out of buried cities
vacuuming ocean floors

It draws earth from earth
spherical
Another planet that comes rolling towards us
nothing in its way

Preparations for the Catastrophe

Preparations for the catastrophe
were a catastrophe
The effort to alert people
has been a catastrophic failure

All attempts to rescue
the innocent
only visited
greater catastrophe
upon
those so thoroughly
visited
by the previous catastrophe

Catastrophe relief
breeds catastrophe
from catastrophe
like salt from the sea
Everywhere a trillion crystal catastrophes
splinter into catastrophic tomorrows
and the ongoing search for a strategy
to stop this cascade short of its full
catastrophic potential
is thought to be
at best catastrophe in the making

What the Albatross Has Round Its Neck

What the albatross has round its neck
is heavy water
is chlorine and mercury
is the two ton cross
and weapons-grade plutonium

What the albatross has round its neck
is the death of fish
the death of sea lions
the extinction of polar bears
the passing of the otter

The weight of it bears down at the back of its neck
like a slow-mo guillotine

The great bird lifts anvil wings
continents-wide
and sinks toward the smeary
sun-weary horizon
its amulet skidding
on the leaden grey sea

Ravine

Invisible the river flows below
till twilight shifts and suddenly I see
above it, a water wraith exposed
a higher river of mist ghostly green —
a sunset river undulant in air
winding on the dark the valley makes.
The only sign that there is water there —
this mist inhabited by birds of prey
who swoop below at frightened fleeing things
in swift long arcing shadows of intent.
Invincible on wings and shadow wings
they hunt the lower current till they're spent
and then arise with eyes and talons bare
or if their claws strike true they light and tear.

On the Way to the Walbran Forest

The forest's high and hems us in both sides.
Above, the sky's a line of pre-dawn gold —
A road to match this one we ride
threading through massive cedars, dark and cold.
And sometimes when we crest a hill we get
a vision through the mist — of the far peak
which overlooks the unseen watershed —
a shepherd king guarding his sheep.
But then as morning comes, the highway veers —
a break between the trees where dawn peeks through
and to our shock the wider scene appears.
These trees are just a strip to block the view.
There's clear-cut valleys, seas of stumps beyond
The mountain scalp stripped bare, the forest gone.

Beasts of Burden

The elephant who's tied beside the trees
could snap her bond and run away with ease
She's held by just a piece of slender string
but she believes her cruel conditioning
and so she waits in thirst and heat of sun
her will asleep, a sullen megaton
of life on hold of dreams held down denied
while strength undreamed of fulminates inside
And while she waits to bear what must be born
her rider stops to haggle and to feed
He's lower caste — he bears the Brahmin's scorn
A life from which he knows he can't be freed
Both victims of belief — of states of mind
Both slaves to habit and to man unkind

Chimp with Organ

A chimp with organ stands atop a tank
and winds the music backwards with a crank

Back to the barrel the old ink is sluiced
restoring aging pages blank and white.
Uncross those tees, de-loop those useless loops
This law, that law, this universal right

Unravel flags, unthread the rebel tongue
as ranks in solemn unison recede
Their legs lift straight from hip to toe as one
as if to say they have no need of knees

Drag back those haughty girls who stride to school
undo the suppositions of their birth
Unbind the land restore the ore to corporate rule
Let hunger up out of the barren earth

A chimp with organ stands atop a tank
and winds the music backwards with a crank

Still Life with Girl Diving

The ocean is fixed
waves stopped far from shore

The mechanical grinding
the stuttering static of it shut off

Surfers fastened to breakers squat and wait
the shrieks of gulls like squeaky wheels silenced

Glued to swells, boats and buoys are frozen mid-bob
fish pressed against rigid waters

Seaweed unable to undulate, the brine inflexible
Everything stuck to everything else

A swimmer motionless in glass, one elbow up
shattered waters half knit back together behind him

Cormorants dashed on their own reflections
Squid brittle in immutable nets

The old sea shanties don't carry, the siren's call stalled
mermaids gagged on their songs

The oil tanker's deadlocked
its anchor stopped just short of the pipeline

Sailors forever still, the sun unsinkable
a red rim crushed flat on the horizon

A girl in a colourful bikini, a rainbow arc in midair
neither of the dock nor of the sea

The Great Canadian Oath of Silence

I will be silent
for our unarmed forces
for the forceless
for incinerated children
who got a good starving first
who caught the long slow sickness first

I will be silent
for mercuric waterways
whose fish can't be eaten

Expect to hear nothing from me
about the unassimilated
about children of the distance
about children seven generations and hence

This is not a day to remind people about promises
yet again
The words deceit genocide treaty complicity
won't get to my lips

I won't speak of
children removed from family
for reasons of poverty
right now nearby
ongoing increasing
more now than ever
children in what they call "care"

I won't say Indigenous children
I will silently support others
in their silence on these issues

I will not argue over language
We need neither correct nor incorrect terms
to say nothing

Your Brand New Bag

It's a petroleum blister
your brand new bag

You are hauling greens
in a little oil bubble

Immortal flesh
of infinite oil

set to spread
to cover all soils

all seas all beaches
They replicate up from underground

White cauls, Jurassic ghosts
mouthing our groceries

choking our birds
clinging to us

hanging from our wrists
like burned skin

Everyone Knows Where They Were When They First Heard about the Death of the World

You wake up
and you catch a passing glimpse of it
on the ticker tape at the bottom of the TV
World dies in its sleep!
You're not sure you saw it right
How long do you have to wait for it to roll by again?
Maybe it would be faster to Google it
Has the world died?
Did the world die last night?

The text comes by again
World Dies in its sleep! No!
It can't be
It was still so young
It was part of your childhood
You grew up listening to the rivers of the world
You remember its solidness
The way it was always there when you put your foot down
The way you could put apartment buildings on it
and grow forests on it
Its spinning, its waters
The way the wind could
flap a flag out and carry
ten thousand gulls
into a single sunset

The grief can't get out of your throat
It's like something has been yanked out of your own insides
It's like the world was part of you.
Your chest, your ribs ache
as though they are going to crack open

That first night is agony
The moon still
circling up there as
though the world hadn't died
strangers holding strangers
animals howling in the darkness
How will we go on without the world?
We must never forget the world
If only we could tell the world
One more time how much we love her

What Is Missing

The sky is a stopped sonnet
dropped on the thirteenth line
its symmetries misaligned
no proper ending to it
It just hangs there aloft
its clouds full of cannon
that can't quite go off
its words going soft
The sky is somehow cut short
truncated, bereft of some essential thing
that being a sky requires
Is it hope? Is it kites? A kiss?
What is missing from the sky? A fist . . .

Monstrosity

We Frankenstein our mangoes
We Dracula the lambs and calves
Murder the herded peoples
our mammal thralls

What is a werewolf compared to us
We outmonster the monsters
Where in the fairy tales
is there anything like the Holocaust

If only our greatest danger
was the Minotaur

The worst that can happen
is that somewhere in the maze
we encounter each other

Peacenik

Is it nonviolence
if all day
my mind is full of fists
if all night
I see you swing from the gallows pole

Is it nonviolence
if I can't stop imagining
exit wound spatters
from various areas of your skull
if I long to do the dance
of kicking in your throat
of scooping out the orbits of your eyes

All day I stride the floor
like a caged panther
I'm a flipbook
of homicides
a carousel of torments

I grasp at happy thoughts
but like razor blades
they slip my grip
I breathe in peace
I breathe out hate
I breathe out holy murder
I breathe out the flaying knife
the breaking wheel
I breathe out slow time
that kills but never quite kills

Hunger Knows No Lockdown

Hunger knows no lockdown
It gets in the wind it leaks into rivers
crossing borders
It waits in the soil
corroding seed

Hunger keeps no distance
It comes in close and gets at the throat
devouring muscle, weighing down the head
Hunger gnaws the bone of the belly
sucks the marrow
and leaves nothing on the plate

Pestilence only aids hunger
Scorched earth feeds it
War makes hunger stronger
With every missile
hunger explodes and burrows in deeper

There is no paralysis for starvation
Famine needs no disguise, no lies
It wears no mask

Its breath is your breath
Its naked face an infant face

Final Comedy Routine

Please refrain from gnawing on your knuckles
Please desist from sucking on your fist
Swallowing air will only make you bloated
and the bloated will be processed last

No plucking every vein —
                                        looking for the lost melody
The coffins I'm afraid are only for the dead
Please refrain from warming children in the shrouds

Those who wanted peace please step over here
Who among you has ever composed a love song?
No writing down the names of the dead
The shelters are not to be used under any circumstances

Suicide will simply not be tolerated
Please report all physicians to the prosecutor

Loving My Enemy

Atrocities are aphrodisiac
Malice melts my heart
I long to cradle
his pilot head
I have only lust
for his trigger finger
I can do nothing but long
for this poisoner of rivers
this despoiler of soils
I live only to be
in the crosshairs
of his most automatic weapon
The need to run and meet the drone
keeps me sleepless

I am no longer half a man
no longer a puzzle
without pieces
The glass heart has found
its shattered shattering other
Love's thread
sews our two edges into one wound
one scar

When he fires burning bullets
I fire back Valentines
If the red rose explodes
from a comrade's back
I apply more and more lipstick

No battlefield can keep us apart
We promise death, division, divorce
but our treaties are broken
We are joined in holy acrimony
Married in murder

Infection Prevention for Murderers

Murderers are advised to keep at least six feet away from intended victims. Projectile murder is safest — bullets, arrows, and drones are ideal for social distancing. Knives must be thrown, not thrust, and should be thoroughly sanitized before reuse. Garottes require dry cleaning. After murdering someone, do not touch your mouth or eyes. Strangulation with bare hands is not considered safe, nor the administration of beatings by fists. Be especially careful not to let victims touch your nose or eyes while begging. Whenever possible, murder from behind to prevent victims screaming directly into your face. A stick at least six feet long is required for pushing victims into threshers or off cliffs. The six-foot rule also applies to lineups for gun stores and torture implement surplus outlets. Torturers should not, in any instance, remove their masks. To assure the efficacy of scrubbing car surfaces after vehicular manslaughter sing the happy birthday song three times. It is advisable to wear single-use disposable plastic gloves when signing execution warrants. If you are murdering people by refusing services, information, medication or nutrition, always wear full-body PPE. Electric chairs must be vigorously sanitized and left for up to ten minutes before reuse.

Help

Use of the word "help" came into question. It was a demeaning term used to signify those who served. *The help.* It whittled humans down to nothing more than their contracted labour and in so doing tainted the word for use in denoting any endeavour to assist. This quickly became a subject for irate discussions and keynote addresses among those who believed themselves in charge of such issues. Soon the word "help" was out of favour in the academy and if used was always done so in finger quotes. Those not yet reached by this linguistic furor would sometimes innocently use the word and suffer the pain of a public shaming. In many cases such people thereafter became silent about issues of concern for fear of using incorrect language. In other cases where the shamed felt unjustly treated, anger and bitterness developed to such a degree that hearts originally open to the injustices done to others hardened.

As the process of public shaming widened in scope disuse of the word filtered down to groups of people who did not necessarily know the very fine points that the earlier discussions had delineated but did know the required behaviour to avoid shaming. Eventually the processes of correction and chiding grew to be so ubiquitous the word was consigned to the ranks of the vilest epithets. At first there were a few notable holdouts, the Paramedics Union, the Society of Nurses, and the League of First Responders all continued to use it in quotes in their literature and textbooks but this caused such an outcry the volumes had to be reprinted and apologies made.

None of this had done much to alter the deep issues of inequity, injustice, prejudice, hunger, and violence in the societal structures that had originally compelled some to assist. One positive result though was that many notables acquired careers writing theses and "popular" tomes on the subject. Among those who definitely did not benefit were the ten children, three dogs, and a nanny all of whom while caught in a house fire screamed "the H word" to no avail as they died of smoke inhalation and severe burns. Though there were many passersby who might have attempted to rescue the children or alert the fire department they were to a person so horrified by this frantic explosion of expletives that they hurried away in disgust.

Idea for Genetic Engineering

What if there were a moral act orgasm —
a new way to come
because you stand up for a just cause
A way to come
if you're whacked by a baton in a protest
A way to come wonderful if you're tear-gassed
and handcuffed

What if we found a gene splice
to make us lust for peace in the streets
like it was the love of our lives
What if only truth could get us hot and bothered

What if there were dirty little booths
on Yonge Street where you could
furtively give huge amounts of coin
to charity
and have an orgasm that just foams your bones

It would be so erotic to be in Doctors without Borders
If you were a pro bono lawyer against Monsanto
you'd hardly be able to walk for the orgasms

We should be re-engineered so that
the only way to really get our rocks off
is to end child poverty on earth

Deglobalized Violin

I

Now that it's *here*
the bow may touch the string

intimately
The very very local

is so important here
Focus on the local

is exquisite and at angles
It is all about a glint instant

in the diamond flow
of the fine crystal frequencies

stroked up by the bow
and in that sense microscopic

in its tone
that a skilled player

may tempt up molecules
melodiously symmetrical

Mutually resonating runs
and long violin tones so human

you'd think we'd found
a trick to transmit ourselves

directly into wood and air
To beam ourselves elsewhere

and while we're away
play our own bones

II

There is sex inside the violin
You can get at it
with the right movement
It will seize you from the centre of the chamber
You'll be stoking eternal orgasm up out of nothingness
Where bow meets string, mind meets the matterless
and the taut void sings

You saw away
There is sex inside the violin
You are going at it maniacally
If it were a tree it would be down by now
But it is the sex in the middle of the violin
and you've got to come at it from every angle
With the right combination of strokes
you'll reach that shriek of nexus
your bow right in the centre of all that wants
needs
wanton like a lioness waiting for the sixth mounting
Like the python when the kid is still crying inside
The violin does not care
The sexual spirit hunger has it
It wants to find the tones
of exquisite torture in telephone lines

To be a saw
sawing
a saw
or a file
filing a
file
would be a good thing
but this stroking of honey
by honey
this rubbing of sugar
with sugar

Shane Swallowed the World

Shane swallowed the world
and it's hurting him
It moves up into his hands
when he speaks
trying to get out
When he gestures
the earth curves into his fingers
close to the surface
The bedrock cracks in his chest
when he speaks
His voice changes like a season
in a second
One minute it hangs like a wet rag
from his chin and quivers
with each blast
and the next it is deep as oak
catching at grief like
gears missing a spoke
the sun bursting wide open
in his throat
like a burning coal swallowed whole
and now from the darkest pit of the soul
finally allowed to glow

Shane gulped down
all the earth's misery and hope
in one shot glass
and he can only get it out now
note by shining note
a pearl at a time
or in long rapids
of words

half sunk half afloat
on a current
of tears at first
and then a second later
a joke
a grin
as he goes on to the next verse
A colossus
reeling in the stars
for a bit of light
His heart a massive
black dam
holding back
night

What Francesca Does to English

You must encounter her by chance
and ask directions
When she sets you straight
she sets the English language straight
shows you the hidden elegance
so close, but for Canadians, alas,
so far away
Perhaps it is her face
its perfect shape, this mouth
that cannot sound a consonant that grates
or grinds — cannot allow a single vowel
to come out half pronounced
or anything but full and rich
— like her lips

A daring youth comes by
points to his cheek
as if she'd kiss
a saucy lout for such a bold request!
She smiles
She's kind
She waves him on —
he dances off —
thrilled to get so close to her
with his attempt

Now she returns to us
a twinkle in her eyes
She smiles and points as she directs
"Via Mercante all the way."
Her jet black hair is huge and gathered high
A wilderness of helixes and spirals

as though someone had drawn
ink from all poetic texts
and spun it into micro coils of ebon thread
infinite but bound —
a manta crown
about her head
A resource for whatever poet's pen
should seek to praise it next
"Gràzie" we say
And she incites
such elegance in me
I bow a bit —
sad to part —
A little torn
but glad to know my tongue
which seemed so recently a little dead
has been so perfectly reborn

Way Too Old

I'm way too old
for the trees

I look at them the same way I did
as a boy

but I forget that I am wrinkled now
I forget that I am ragged

To the roses I'm a relic
To young ladies I am part of the ruin

of the earth
I am way too old for the lakes

or the fossils in the mountains, I flirt with the sky
thinking I'm still some young stud

but my bones creak with each gesture
My neck strains to look up

My worst nightmare is
not that I'll fall and shit my pants

but that the stars flirting back
might actually ask me to dance

Keyhole Telescopic

There's nothing so titillating to suddenly see
as the bottoms of the stars
To gaze up under stellar dresses into dark funk
and catch them winking as they stride
see them twinkling in and out of sight
the pornographic lens angled high
for just a glimpse of between-thigh nebulae
The upper hook of the un-slung moon
lolling about up there head rocked back
straddling the naked planetary curve
twisting off into forbidden orbits
never knowing they're observed
never sensing the erotic lens, the antennae
Peeping Tom eyes can't keep off the sky

Adoration

When you see me bite my tongue
it's because I'm not saying

you are a river
where everything beautiful reflects

I see the sky in you
the heron flying over

I understand complete
fealty

The urge to genuflect
so instinctive

I can hardly stand straight
The urge to proclaim your beauty to you

ever present
always almost out

Black night needs stars moons
it fades in morning light

But your skin
only shines darker in the dawn

This adoration is so deep
I must've been a peasant a million times

But this is not an age
for adorers

I hope my eyes don't shout
I hope my smile is not too much a sign

Or if you're telepathic
and have a complementary urge to mine

perhaps my silent wonder
pleases you as I walk by

Head

Symmetrical shapes
mostly vees
That's the way I remember her best

Half-fallen titan
vertical to the knees
sprawled on her back
on the bed
The chin beyond
the mirror curve
of breasts
swayed to the sides
groaning like a violin

And I am the hand on the bow
the tongue on the saxophone
I am the one kneeling low
doing my best to please

And yes
I confess
counting myself blessed

For Francesca with a Broken Heart

A heart is made to be broken
like a bicycle helmet
that cracks on impact
instead of your head.

The heart splits
or balloons out
and pushes you back
whole and away from impact.
It takes the blow.
A passion fuse
that pops in overload.

When your heart breaks
remember —
you have been saved.
When you're up against a post
pounding with your fist, "No! No! No!"
understand you've been blown off a terrible course.
The guard rail has kept you back
from the abyss of deeper and deeper.

Your safety heart
took the big dark weight of loss
and shunted it to the side.

When you're bucking in the bed
biting the sheets
trying to strangle that scream
remember:

this is missing a calamity
this is what it's like to get away.

Thigh

If I saw your naked thigh
one of many
on some bikini beach stroll
I might hardly turn my head

Or if in a Fellini scene
among a tangle of limbs
one naked thigh was yours
I can't say I'd notice

Even if we lived close enough
to walk together
in thin summer shorts
a passing glance down
would probably suffice

But yesterday
sitting knees up in your chair
adjusting
your camera on Zoom
a close-up
along one monumental thigh
suddenly appeared
and disappeared
and my heart thumped
into the back of my ribs
so hard

B.A.S.D.

Beauty Attention Surfeit Disorder . . .
So good to finally have a name for it
It's your brain's tendency to blur borders
that brings on your unwelcome staring fits
You see beauty and your eyes lock in tight
Attention! Attention! The hunt is on
You're caught up in a neolithic drive
and all attempts to put your blinders on
are frozen in her glare — that's your malaise
A classic case of B.A.S.D.
It's not your fault you can't avert your gaze
But diagnosis doesn't mean relief
Still when women sneer, poor you, the shame runs deep —
"It's not a sickness, man," you say, "I'm just a creep."

Sonnet of Many Skins

A cotton skin castoff, a skin of sky
A Joseph's coat of streaked and mottled puce
The skin of steel I slip inside to fly
A patterned snakeskin made of thought torn loose
A frozen skin of cellophane I hide
A flag skin rippling out for any wind
A paper skin whose symbols I transcribe
A skin beneath them all — my unborn twin
The skin of stars my fingers burn to touch
A skin of time its clock notched with each breath
The ancient skin's three-legged walk, a crutch
of bones to pitch the many-layered tent
in which the poet binds his song to soul
as though life had some single path — some goal

Whinge

When I am grabbed in envy's heavy fist
and held to feel the estimate, the pinch,
of reputation's arbitrary inch
(deduced by who's not on the latest list)
When other poets stand to take the prize
and I am uninvited to the dance
and then I see the jury bound by ties
of friendship, which they claim are just by chance
I snort and hork, expel the green of phlegm
I rage and whinge, and poison fills my mind
I go and find their books and sneer at them
until among them, shining, I find mine
I open it and glory fills my eyes
and I am calm — in grace — this is the prize

It's Not Your Fault

It's not your fault. It's not my fault. It's chance.
So why compound our suffering with blame?
We're all just pawns of circumstance.

Put your fingers on a pond — they dance.
If my reflection's ruined by the rain
It's not your fault. It's not my fault. It's chance.

The infant shrieks; the father raves and rants.
It hurts so much, why maximize the pain?
We're all just pawns of circumstance.

The child is too. I see it in his stance.
He cannot get that message through his brain.
It's not your fault. It's not my fault. It's chance.

We sleep, we wake, we breakup in a trance.
Why probe our wounds and make them bleed again?
It's not your fault. It's not my fault. It's chance.
We're all just pawns of circumstance.

Over-Reacher

I'm not an over-reacher by intent
      It's just there's more than those few far-off stars
you pointed out to me when I was ten
      I held them hissing in my palms, look — scars
and higher scars that say I reached beyond
      That say I dove through stars and streaked my flesh
as though a god burned maps of rivers there
      Arriving in the end at something less
than that for which I made my hasty leap
      If I had only settled for a lower rung
If I'd aimed true and low when I was young
      I might not now be sunk so goddamn deep
But why berate myself? I found my voice
      I had to sing, I simply had no choice.

Nothingness in Us

Sure, I believed, there is only matter.
The rest is physics. The rest is up to us —
Freeze-frame it or dance it into tatters.
Either way we're bound to wind up dust.
The world of things (we never get enough!)
will stave it off. All you have to do
is stay afloat on mounting waves of stuff.
Waves however also serve to block the view
on emptiness and thus affirm the lie
that bone and skin are all the soul can trust.
Best we deny the nothingness in us.
But when it comes — the insubstantial tide —
we cry and grasp each other, straws made flesh
"If we lose ourselves," we cry, "nothing's left."

The Name Is Bomb, James Bomb

Because our countries have a sacred bomb
I offer you my bomb, a bomb of blood
The family bomb, I give my word and bomb
Invest in bombs: the price of bombs is up —

Buy stocks and bombs, get housing bombs, war bombs,
The bomb of co-religion, bombs of race
The special bomb that daughters have with moms
Not cheap junk bombs that blow up in your face

Investment bombs build our economy
We find ourselves bound by a common bomb
The movie has some great male bombing scenes.
The kind of bomb that Rumi had with Shams

The bomb of those who struggle and give birth
The human bomb, the surly bombs of earth

Thought/Fat Meme Splice Sonnet

My head is full of fats. Disturbing fats.
Sometimes I have a thousand fats at once
Dark secret fats that shame me. Dirty fats.
I shudder at the fat. The fat that counts.

I am absorbed in fat. Intrusive fats.
Junk fat. So who made you the fat police?
Just hold that fat. Sometimes I have gay fats.
One day I hope my fat will be at peace.

It's just the fat of you, the very fat of you,
my love. It's fuel for fat. It's food for fat.
I don't subscribe to that outdated school
of fat. I'm more in tune with Nietzsche's fat.

I'm tortured by the fats that sink and whirl.
If you can change your fats you change the world.

In the Future

In the future there will be so many new synonyms that people speaking English fluently will be entirely unable to understand other people speaking English. All poetry at that time will be written in the English you don't understand.

In the future instead of war games kids will play conflict resolution expert. Football will be mainly negotiation.

In the future we'll have the equivalent of marriage counsellors for every relationship in our lives. A whole new layer of middle people.

In the future people who have made billions of dollars from poetry deals will give a huge cash prize to the "best" Canadian arms maker.

In the near future a new law will allow us to get reverse mortgages on our grandchildren's homes and our great great grandchildren's homes and so on.

In the future when chickens are a protected and endangered species there will still be a lucrative market in illegal chickens fuelled by superstitious Westerners who believe chicken soup can cure the common cold.

In the future there will still be freedom of religion but religion will consist of already proven scientific facts which have to be taken on faith without question or any further experimentation.

In the future good-hearted time travellers will try to rescue the people of the past. Every child who ever died, all the starved and denied, tragic lovers killed in futile wars, one by one, will be rescued and brought to the present. They will even come back to save you and me from whatever we die of. Their motto will be "All death is premature."

In the future long after there are no more rivers people will still build bridges because of their beauty.

In the future people will be so mobile no one will ever see anyone they've seen previously. Everyone will be a stranger.

In the very distant future we will develop a much more advanced World Wide Web that enables us to communicate clearly with the person in the room right beside us.

My Women Named Marsha Kirzner Thing

I have a Marsha Kirzner in every major city across the continent.
I am obsessed with women named Marsha Kirzner. In Dallas I
have a Marsha Kirzner who leans over one side so that her hair
hangs straight down. I call her the willow Marsha Kirzner. And
there is a Marsha Kirzner who comes out to train stations in the
Prairies with me and has straight sex through the most golden of
the wheat fields. This Marsha Kirzner must be timed right but she
abhors clocks and calendars. I have a Marsha Kirzner in Winnipeg
who loves the cold but hates duvets. She likes to sleep on top of
sheets with the windows open half-naked. I have never managed
to spend the whole night with her yet. Marsha Kirzner the cook
from St. Louis is a favourite of mine. I try to get gigs in St. Louis
entirely for her deep-dish pizza. I have fourteen women named
Marsha Kirzner in small towns between Calgary and Lethbridge
but they are all shy and have expressly asked to be left out of any
poems containing their names, so . . . I have a Marsha Kirzner in
the mountains. I would stay with her there forever but I hate the
mountains and she will never leave them. I have a unique Marsha
Kirzner in Vancouver. I stay with her in the best room at the Sylvia
and we complain about the sea — which we both feel has let us
down. Marsha Kirzners of the island abound. The one in Victoria
always has another house. She insists upon seashores. She insists on
treks to fabulous forests. I am not counting the ones called Marsha
Kirshner. Phonic spelling of the name is key for me. In New York
I actually have six Marsha Kirzners. I find them at poetry readings.
You can usually get at least one Marsha Kirzner at the *Imagine
Mosaic* in Central Park. If you hear a long row of beeping cars
impatiently trying to proceed past an intersection — go to the car
at the front — if it has paused to let some pedestrian creep across
illegally — that is likely a Marsha Kirzner. Certain tricks work
on the majority of them. They all are insecure about their clothes.
They all herd regrets into small stalls. There are some with hidden

talents — monster hidden talents, genius hidden talents that they dare not acknowledge due to some curse or amnesia. I can't figure it out. Most of them are under a spell. Usually there has been some magnetics work done. They are to a person extremely gentle. If you ever need care. Find a Marsha Kirzner. The problem for me is this: I love them all. There's none of them I have a merely shallow relationship with. I dread hurting any one of them but my nightmares arc full of strange conjunctions. Marsha Kirzner conventions. A four-hour exposé called *Women Named Marsha Kirzner: What They Don't Know.* How many more Marsha Kirzners will I fall for before I'm interrogated? Before I am asked some kind of piercing question? "I swear" I'll answer with utter honesty. "I love no one so deeply, in all the world as Marsha Kirzner."

Nothing Made This Love Inevitable

Nothing made this love inevitable
until I saw you

sitting in a circle
in the daycare centre

a deterministic moment
Incredible odds were against it

but I knew I had time
and talent

so I waited
for which in retrospect

I now believe
I was fated

Nothing made this love irreversible
till we both leaned forward and kissed

over a small table
with a carafe of white wine

between us
The taste of your lips

entirely unforeseen
took me by surprise

What were the prophets thinking
No one predicted this

Eitan Means Strong
(for Eitan Lebo, June 3, 2011–May 27, 2019)

Where two played now one plays alone
your birthday candles never again to know the arc
of flame before your blasts of celebrated age
They'll burn for others now —
not you in your beauty
not you and your talent
The pond's reflected sky no longer to be opened
by joyous hands where once you swam
Who knows what you'd have brought to troubled times
when you became a man
how many hearts other than ours
you might have warmed

Me, with my memory
destroyed wondering what you were
searching photographs for clues
clutching void air to remember a song never to be sung
A place in my chest like a grave
where once a child was hugged and held

Cruel leukemia goes on without you
bringing more agony, more heartbreak
The pain, the fear you braved
a grown man would dread
let alone a child
What might such courage have brought
this frightened world, this world bereft

You'll never quite be eight now
you'll always be a child
Your little brother growing beyond you
one chair empty
one of two swings hanging still

Too Much Like Heaven
(for Eitan Lebo and Rafiki Cruise)

O child why did you go
Why we couldn't keep you here
I'll never know
What you might have been
in your own tomorrow — oh
I guess it's too much like heaven
too much like heaven
too much like heaven
for a world like this to know

Dear child I hear your song
forever in my memory
I'll sing along
All the joy we might have had
if love had let you grow
I guess it's too much like heaven
too much like heaven
too much like heaven
for a world like this to know

Long as these cold winds blow
I'll allow these bitter tears to flow
How we might have laughed today
unknown to sorrow

Oh child our love is long
I see your eyes so pure and clear
I must be strong
What you might have been
if we never let you go
I guess it's too much like heaven

too much like heaven
too much like heaven
for a world like this to know

TOO MUCH LIKE HEAVEN

Words and Music by Robert Priest and Allen Booth

87

Clock of One Word

There is no past
It is the present in disguise

The ever present present
piling up on itself

always moving the goalposts
shuffling its card to the front of the deck

The surface tension at the tip
of the big wave pushing us

dragging us along with it
ever forward

If we walk back into the waves
it's the present about our knees

If we throw a heart at history
it's the raw present that beats

futile
on the beach

All previous deaths are present
in this one death

The clock of one word
"now"

or on bad days
"not then"

not ever "then"
again

You Were There

You were there
when the stars fell down
and burned my eyes

And when the thirst was at its worst
you stayed without water
to be with me

I felt it in your touch
I felt it in your care
There was never a time
when I was unaware
of your presence
beside me

You were there
when I was nowhere
you walked beside me in the abyss
And when I stood impoverished
with nothing to declare
you were there

Every place I left
you left with me
And when I got anywhere
it was like you had preceded me
It was like you had always been there
awaiting my arrival

Against Love

We hold each other
We align ourselves

Touching toe tips
and brow tops

We pitch the tent
of our own bones

our own flesh
Love leans against love —

a teepee
and love inside

is the fire
Love leans into love

a sail into sunlight
a river into rain

We ride the boat
love makes of us

We know the prayer kiss
and bliss is our way

Love holds up love
like a lantern

and looks love
in the face

beaming

Two Sheets on a Line

My eyes are bright but I am dark inside
A strip of shadow hung upon a line
I can't get free alone god knows I've tried
but there is only midnight in my mind
I stare in vain. I might as well be blind
I have no hope. I'm lost in nameless fear
I grope through pitch with hands that cannot find
a remedy — until . . . I sense you near
You're sensitive wet silk the sun shines through
And when the wind is hot and blows so much
it causes my wet sheet beside to touch
my skin goes all transparent — yours does too
We cling together and my darkness dissipates
And now that I can see it clear my fear abates

Caregiver

Who pushes you away and out of view
Who barely lets you sleep before you wake
Who tells you you are no one — number none
and keeps you churning dry without a break

Whose grating voices carp and criticize
berating you for all you have not done
while circles deepen underneath your eyes
imprinted by a grey life without sun

Who cuts your share and never gives you due
and keeps you working even when you're sick
Who rides so hard — and keeps on whipping you
like some poor harnessed horse stuck in a ditch

You give such care to everybody else
Why not to that poor tired soul — yourself

Information

The void it's thought expanded evenly
except those parts where there were uh . . . mistakes
Odd catch-wells of increasing gravity
where matter forms and gathers till it breaks
There, crystal chains were set to agitate
against the aimless ways of entropy
dividing they began to procreate
and make the information making me
Once we were bright, exploded from a star
across the night, the opposite of dark,
we shone and somehow here we are
With burning brands in hand we weave our mark
against this loss — the sun-dividing sun
We're not apart beloved we are one

Jade

Will love decline with time just like our flesh?
      Like us will all its joints begin to creak
      and ache with every act of tenderness?
Does love decay and fade as we grow weak

with age and all that clinging in the night
      to wind up wrinkled, poor, enfeebled, cold?
      I hold you trembling scared before the light
that shows us greying, on the verge of old

But even in my fear I catch my breath
      to see that ageless jade shine in your eyes
      And in their gaze I lose my fear of death
for love just adds to love it doesn't die

It lives in every breath of love that's ever been
It blows away the years and leaves us evergreen

For Marsha Taking Smaller Portions

There is too much of you
you tell me
taking smaller portions
weaning yourself off rice

But you're just large boned
and you have a big heart
Don't lose weight there

Sometimes the world is so heavy
but limiting your starches — what will that do

If you have a bit of a temple belly
that is more of you to love
that is more warmth in the night
another luscious curve
to ease the eyes

Why deny yourself
to deny others

I know full well
you carry heavy sorrow
Worries weigh you down

Come to bed goddess
let me help you lose them

In Order To Be Silent

We have to let the words destroy themselves
And that means we will have to numb our hearts
and wait. It's up to us and no one else.
We need to listen as they're torn apart.
Like Noah's beasts untethered in the ark
in shifting cells inside the lexicons
each one impressed on others in the dark
must leave behind as though it's branded on
some momentary meaning of its mark.
But ever after they will flap and chafe
to tear themselves like Furies from such rock.
They break at such a rate it is not safe
to even whisper, let alone to write.
It's best we lie here quiet in the night.

I Find My Way In

The gift is a closed house
a sealed off heart
the gift is a shutdown face
and I must find my way in
I let a word rise in my chest
feel its richness
the word is hope
its skin thin
it releases
treasure into me
Through the pinhole pen it wriggles
onto the page
The gift is language
one word hooking up with another
one word hauling another out of the mine
I allow the secret life
take in the children and their cries
animals shelter in me
The gift is sun
I turn the key
and stars river through me
love rises buoyant in my blood
passions emerge
and in the passions words
and in the words birds
and in the birds song flight sky
they all take me in
I am pain to them and grief
but inside the pain
inside the grief
a field
a tree a nest

They knock, the wind knocks
my door is dissolving
my eyes wide
my skin porous
The world pushes past
Its gift is spirit
and inside spirit
awareness
I knock and knock again
I open the door that is not a door
to a self that is not a self
I am the poverty of it
the sorrow and the anger
Come in I say
and they enter me
and I know nothing
and nothing is the gift
but inside nothing
I sense a presence
perhaps it is a universe
perhaps it is a word
for the unsayable
I slip into my body
and my body slips into me
If the word is *home*
I don't know how to say it
but you come naked
no hard shell
no in or out

your beauty means nothing to you
you reach me
touch a surface like water
and you whisper
the word in my ear

the word is *thanks*

Progression of Buts

I shouldn't be saying this but —
Typically the majority stand for it but —
They assumed we'd go on being quiet but —
They said that moral courage was at a minimum but —
They thought we'd go on stunned in the grey TV glow but —
They thought we were flies on the screen forever but —
Even we believed we had no wings, no grandeur but —
They thought our outrage was dead but —
There are supposed to be limits
on how long you can push it push it push it but but but —
We thought we'd lost each other but —
They believed that silence was assent forever but —
It looked like it was going to be World War III but —
They said that faith was not a well, not a flow, not a channel but —
I was telling everybody don't count on me, I can't be relied upon but —
They're going to tell us we're not brave but —
They're going to push the negative but —
They said there was no buttress but —
No resistance but —
No insistence but —
No victory but —

I Slip My Will

With a dark mark
my intent is known

All my power contracts
smaller than a pupil

to provide one ink drop
of ocean

more countable
than blessings

And I may have to walk
a mile for this

I may have to stand in line
with hundreds

fixing the bullseye
firmly in mind

every mark for now
a sacred star compressed

a massive black dot
telescoped

to a tiny circumference
of suffrage

Explosive
secret or not

I fold it in upon itself
and slip my will into the slot

Materials for an Interconnected Nest

That last straw
the one that broke the camel's back
to weave forgiveness in the nest

The straw I grasp so I won't drown
One filament of gosling down
The straw I pluck from a scarecrow's breast
A shred of bark for sturdiness

A feather that could knock me down
to lend this nest resilience

For wellness weave in binder's twine
and a slender stem of eglantine

From the dog that bit me take one hair
to build in memory and care

A shred of paper cast aside
by a poet in distress
will give this nest both art and strength

Moon twine, star string, thread of dream
For happiness a slip of stream
Milkweed silk woven well
A speck of yarn for tales to tell

Some earth-wet clay from hallowed ground
with spiderweb to bind it round

For righteousness, courageousness
some strands of hair the west wind lifts
from those who gather to protest

A strand of thought for consciousness

And one thread from my lover's dress
for tenderness for faithfulness

In-Body Experience

Different atoms every day
I exchange chemicals
old lamps for new
The smile I had yesterday
was someone else's smile a year ago
My constant love is for a woman
who is a different woman moment by moment
My hands are not my hands I don't own them
In seven years cell by cell
they'll be replaced entirely
My childhood face is long gone
some of it part seagull now
part Frisbee part cannonball
My heart a design for a heart
I'm not my skeleton
not now not yesterday
The tiny fetal bones I had
show up piecemeal in health foods
in mineral baths
an elephant's tusk
My infant teeth are ground down gone
All that breath breathed in want
expelled in scream
was never mine
I'm a borrower a lender
a sand sculpture
My eyes neural ghosts
The palms I soothe you with
I got from the wind
Lips that touch your lips
once were leaves
once were molluscs

Even these words
leak out their meanings
absorbing others
Each instant
a new tongue
a mouth made of many mouths
repurposed ions
fields of energy

Who is this wind full of leaves
who is this night made of rain
Everything formed us
everything brought us here
everything temporary
assembled the hands
we hold together
The lips that whisper
"stay."

Smiles

It's the world off course
with a sudden swerve
a toothless baby-smile
and something in the ankles goes parabolic
a meadow of smile flowers slowly opening
a flock of smiles like wide-winged water birds all rising at once
smiles that don't care what you think about teeth
or the tilting back of the head as though to something in the sky

Millions of micro smiles crimp the edges of the eyes
and warp wide open
smiles that go all the way around
and meet in the middle of the forehead
curved space-time smirk-smiles

What happens to the clothesline when you move the poles closer
what happens to the roof when the rain is too heavy
the way the water bends in on high-pressure days
the new moon on its back, almost up out of the pond
mystic in the linear mind

Detached smiles that are not cups
that can never be bells
that are not butterflies
or parentheses
mouth-mismatching lipstick smiles
boomerang smiles whipping back for a re-smile
smile kissing when one smile kisses another

Come, smile Midas,
lie in the hammock of smile belly
radiating smile-memory
that most reliable curve
your mirth arc

Bend it, twist it
propagate the smile meme
and see how it carries on
the smile-brain amygdala-grin
smiles we can't prevent
miles and miles of exponential smiles
bending gratitude into beauty

Go Free and Gentle

Go free and gentle into that good night
There comes a time for life to slip away
Go clear into the everlasting light

Wise women at their end give up the fight
Because their hearts accept this ending they
Go free and gentle into that good night

Poor men, their last breath come, who know what height
The tide must rise to lift them on a wave
Go clear into the everlasting light

Lost men who grasped at stars to steer them right
And learned that darkness also knows the way
Go free and gentle into that good night

Old women close to death whose eyes shine bright
See day is done, release their souls and fade
Go clear into the everlasting light

And you beloved here for your last flight
Arise, and fly with wings of wind I pray
Go free and gentle into that good night
Go clear into the everlasting light

Micropoems

Inhumanity in humanity

∞∞∞

Injustice in justice

∞∞∞

All crowds tend toward mobness

∞∞∞

Love is blind but hate has telescopic sights

∞∞∞

At what distance do the rings become part of the bullseye?

∞∞∞

The right hand doesn't know what the right hand is doing

∞∞∞

The true outsiders are the homeless, the animals

∞∞∞

No one is no one

∞∞∞

The behated

∞∞∞

You love some you loathe some

∞∞∞

Life liberty and the pursuit of young black men and women

∞∞∞

Of all materials used by the ancients to ensure the longevity of their edifices it is the glass ceilings which have best withstood the test of time

∞∞∞

A farewell to arms dealers

∞∞∞

Ask not for whom the drone falls

∞∞∞

When we fight darkness with darkness it just gets darker

∞∞∞

Why seek out the needle of offence in a haystack of good intentions?

∞∞∞

Shame is the new fame

∞∞∞

Those who will say anything usually have nothing to say

∞∞∞

Science is all question question question and religion is all answer
answer answer

ooooo

When one bum fluff calls another bum fluff "a lightweight"

ooooo

When I am slighted it never feels slight

ooooo

Either either or or

ooooo

Neither neither nor nor

ooooo

The ismists

ooooo

Respect your youngers

ooooo

I'm so old I have an inner adult

ooooo

I'm waiting for whatever supersedes the super seeds

ooooo

The worst thing dominoes can do is stand together

ooooo

Count your blessings — just don't count mine

ooooo

When will the beloved be loved?

ooooo

What does the phoenix gain by suicide?

ooooo

If you pray you are the pray-er

ooooo

The devil only gets to do evil when people close their eyes to pray

ooooo

The reason love gets deeper and deeper is so we can keep falling in it

ooooo

It is easier for a broken heart to pour itself out

ooooo

Physics is the absolute morality of matter

ooooo

It's not time that passes
It's we who pass
Civilizations pass

oooooo

History proceeds by normalizing the grotesque

oooooo

It was humankind that led to human kindness

oooooo

Our angels are each other

oooooo

The devil speaks in legalese

oooooo

Nothing happens that doesn't happen to you

oooooo

It was the guilty who invented forgiveness

oooooo

Thanking anyone is a way of thanking the universe

oooooo

You don't have to be self-centred to get yourself centred

oooooo

Not one person with a properly controlled mind has ever
complained about mind control

oooooo

All thinking is magical thinking

∞∞∞

No one hates laughter more than the ridiculous

∞∞∞

If only starvation could eat indifference

∞∞∞

It was human wrongs that led to human rights

∞∞∞

Apeakoilypse

∞∞∞

Telempathy

∞∞∞

The statusphere

∞∞∞

Whether you are a believer or not the long green gongs
of goddesses still ring in you

∞∞∞

We all come from the same hood — womanhood

∞∞∞

Love is a many-gendered thing

oooo

Transphobia is a choice!

oooo

I strive for outer peace

oooo

Let the world be the peace it wants to see in me

oooo

Prophets see into the future but poets see into the present

oooo

Recite like someone is listening

oooo

One moment in the present is worth all of time in the past

oooo

Poets are the unacknowledged poets of the world

oooo

Poetry is the spell and the magic too

oooo

A Toast at Midnight

Here's to the life we find
in what was left for dead
Here's to redemption
however whenever

I raise my glass
to the water
where we thought
there was an empty well

To the hand we touch
when we're reaching for a stone

Here's to the work of faith
that keeps it going
when the last effort has failed
and the next not yet begun

I drink to the questions we get
when we finally find one answer

To hope that is the wind
lifting dreams aloft
when jackboots squashed them in the mud
when the lash fell on slavery's back

I raise my glass to the courage it takes
to be yourself anyway
and let others do the same

May we be at peace with the experiences of our lives

May our evils fade
and our good works outlast us

May our challenges be the making of us

May we always keep a place in our hearts
for the promise of peace

Acknowledgements

I would like to thank the people of Canada and Ontario who, through their agencies, the Canada Council and the Ontario Arts Council, have generously assisted the writing of these poems with various grants.

For their devoted assistance in helping me through a very hard time in the middle of writing this book I am sincerely grateful to Marsha Kirzner, Allen Booth, David Hines, Bob Cohen, Carol Priest, John Adames, Peter Priest, Ellie Kirzner, Joanne Kirzner, Howie Vernon, Michael Kirzner, Natasha Graham, Ginny McFarlane, Cindy Grief, George Kerr, Daniel Kirzner-Priest, Eli KP William, Eleanor Cruise, and Blair Packham. Also again big thank you to the citizens of Ontario for their wisdom in funding the Ontario Health Insurance Plan.

Some of these poems have appeared in the following journals: *The Quarantine Review*, *Train*, *Literature for the People*, *The Joy of Travel* anthology, *Thule*, *Shot Glass Journal*, *Poetry Pause*, *Poemdemic*, *Amazing Stories*, *BeZine*, *The New Quarterly*, *First of the Month*, *Devour*, *Better than Starbucks*, and *Poetry Hall*.

An audio version of the poem "Deglobalized Violin," with violin accompaniment by Phoebe Tsang, is available on my album *Baam!*

The sonnet "On the Way to the Walbran Forest" appeared previously in *The Wolf Is Back*.

For their assistance in reading early drafts of these poems and supplying comments, I want to thank John Adames, Allen Booth, J.R. Colombo, Karen Alkali-Gut, Heather Ferguson, Maria Jacketti, Marsha Kirzner, Max Layton, Michael Rothenberg, Alison Stone, and Eli KP William. Also, big thanks to my long-time editor, Michael Holmes, and to my so-much-more-than-just-a-copy-editor, Emily Schultz.

The photo on the front cover of this book was taken by my father, Edward Priest. The woman is my mother, Beatrice Priest. I am the smaller of the two children, and my brother Peter is the other child. The river is the Thames.

A literary poet and fabulist in the tradition of Neruda and Mayakovsky, a composer of lush love poems, a singer-songwriter, a widely quoted aphorist, a children's poet and novelist, Robert Priest is a mainstay of the literary/spoken word/music circuit both in Canada and abroad.

His words have been quoted in the *Farmer's Almanac*, debated in Ontario Legislature, sung on *Sesame Street*, turned into a #1 hit song, posted in Toronto's transit system, broadcast on MuchMusic, released on numerous CDs, quoted by politicians, and widely published in textbooks and anthologies.

People's Poet Robert Priest is the author of fourteen books of poetry, three plays, four novels, lots of musical CDs, and one hit song. His 2008 book *Reading the Bible Backwards* peaked at number two on the Canadian poetry charts, its sales exceeded only by those of Leonard Cohen. *Rosa Rose*, a book of children's verse in praise of inspirational figures, won a Silver Moonbeam award in the U.S. and was an honourable mention for The Lion and the Unicorn Award for Excellence in North American Poetry. Its sequel, *The Wolf Is Back,* won the 2017 Golden Moonbeam award. A newly released album of songs and spoken word pieces, *Love is Hard*, is available on Spotify and YouTube. He is also the author of the Young Adult fantasy trilogy Spell Crossed.

For more see: *robertpriest.org*

This book is also available as a Global Certified Accessible™ (GCA) ebook. ECW Press's ebooks are screen reader friendly and are built to meet the needs of those who are unable to read standard print due to blindness, low vision, dyslexia, or a physical disability.

At ECW Press, we want you to enjoy our books in whatever format you like. If you've bought a print copy just send an email to ebook@ecwpress.com and include:

- the book title
- the name of the store where you purchased it
- a screenshot or picture of your order/receipt number and your name
- your preference of file type: PDF (for desktop reading), ePub (for a phone/tablet, Kobo, or Nook), mobi (for Kindle)

A real person will respond to your email with your ebook attached. Please note this offer is only for copies bought for personal use and does not apply to school or library copies.

Thank you for supporting an independently owned Canadian publisher with your purchase!